ANTISEMITISM
WHAT EVERY CHRISTIAN NEEDS TO KNOW AND HOW TO COUNTER IT

DR. SUSAN MICHAEL
USA DIRECTOR
INTERNATIONAL CHRISTIAN EMBASSY JERUSALEM

Antisemitism: What Every Christian Needs to Know and How to Counter It

by Susan M. Michael
Email: embassy.publishers@icejusa.org
Web: www.embassypublishers.org

Copyright © 2023 Susan Michael

Embassy Publishers
PO Box 332974
Murfreesboro, TN 37133-2974

All rights reserved. No part of this book may be reproduced in any form, stored in a retrieval system, or transmitted in any form by any means—electronic, mechanical, photocopy, recording, or otherwise—without permission from the publisher, except as permitted by US copyright law.

Unless otherwise indicated, all Scripture quotations are from the New King James Version®. Copyright © 1982 by Thomas Nelson. Used by permission. All rights reserved.

ISBN: 979-8-9881386-0-1-7
Digital ISBN: 978-0-9839374-5-6

For permissions contact: embassy.publishers@icejusa.org

Editorial: Susan Michael, Tricia Miller; Copyeditor: Karen Engle
Cover design: Peter Ecenroad
Formatting: Nancy Schimp

Printed in the United States of America

First they came for the socialists,
and I did not speak out—
because I was not a socialist.

Then they came for the trade unionists,
and I did not speak out—
because I was not a trade unionist.

Then they came for the Jews,
and I did not speak out—
because I was not a Jew.

Then they came for me,
and there was no one left to speak for me.

Martin Niemöller
German Lutheran pastor and theologian

CONTENTS

Introduction 1

What Is Antisemitism? 3

History of Antisemitism 5

Antisemitism and Christianity 11

Antisemitism in the United States 19

What Can You Do? 27

The International Christian Embassy Jerusalem 29

Resources 30

Free Resource 32

INTRODUCTION

Antisemitism is surging around the world. It is at epidemic levels throughout the Middle East where Jew-hatred is entrenched in everyday life. Europe is at pre-Holocaust levels due to far right parties and an influx of immigrants from Muslim countries. And the United States is experiencing a surge on the internet, on college campuses, and in both the far right and progressive political movements.

According to a 2014 study, 25 percent of the world's population—1.1 billion people—hold antisemitic views, even though 70 percent of those surveyed had never met a Jew. Thirty-five percent had never heard of the Holocaust, and of those who had, one-third thought it was either a myth or greatly exaggerated. The study also showed that the highest percentage of populations holding antisemitic views are found in the Middle East.[1]

An Anti-Defamation League survey conducted in 2019 of 18 European countries discovered about one in four Europeans harbor "pernicious and pervasive attitudes

---

1 *Anti-Defamation League*, "Poll of over 100 Countries Finds More Than One-Quarter of Those Surveyed Infected with Anti-Semitic Attitudes," 13 May 2014.

toward Jews."[2] And a January 2023 study published by The London Centre for the Study of Contemporary Antisemitism in partnership with the Anti-Defamation League and the National Opinion Research Center at the University of Chicago revealed the number of Americans harboring extensive antisemitic prejudice has doubled since 2019, reaching the "highest levels in decades."[3] Interestingly, the report showed a strong correlation between anti-Israel sentiments and antisemitism, with the younger, more progressive generation being particularly susceptible to this.[4]

Antisemitism is not just a Jewish problem and, if unchecked, is a threat to society at large. It is often described as an early-warning system—a canary in the mineshaft—alerting us to hateful movements that can threaten all of us. When Hitler unleashed antisemitism and built the Nazi movement on hatred of Jews, he plunged the world headlong on a path of destruction. Not only were 6 million Jews exterminated but some 50 million people died in World War II.

Christians have a moral obligation to withstand hatred and violence directed toward any group, including Jews. But our responsibility goes beyond that. Knowing the history of centuries of church-sanctioned antisemitism that paved the way for the Holocaust, we particularly need to stand with the Jewish people in their modern battle against this evil.

The Evangelical Christian demographic in America has the political and moral weight to push back against this evil invasion of our society. We must learn how to come against its influence vocally, politically, and prayerfully.

---

2 *Anti-Defamation League,* "ADL Global Survey of 18 Countries Finds Hardcore Anti-Semitic Attitudes Remain Pervasive," 15 November 2019.
3 *Anti-Defamation League*, "Antisemitic Attitudes in America: Topline Findings," 12 January 2023.
4 *World Israel News*, "Whopping Majority of Americans Believe in Antisemitic Tropes, New Poll Finds," January 2023.

WHAT IS ANTISEMITISM?

Antisemitism is hatred of or bigotry toward Jews. The term "antisemitism" was coined in the late 1800s to refer to the opposition of the Jewish people. At the time, antisemitism was viewed positively because hatred against Jews was so widespread in society. In a post-Holocaust world, antisemitism is finally being seen for what it is—a dangerous ideology of hate that must be stopped.

The International Holocaust Remembrance Alliance (IHRA), of which the United States is a member, adopted a non-legally binding "working definition" of antisemitism on May 26, 2016. The US State Department uses this working definition and has encouraged other governments and international organizations to use it as well:

> Antisemitism is a certain perception of Jews, which may be expressed as hatred toward Jews. Rhetorical and physical manifestations of antisemitism are directed toward Jewish or non-Jewish individuals and/or their property, Jewish community institutions, and religious facilities.

The IHRA recommends using the spelling "antisemitism" rather than "anti-Semitism" to dispel the idea that there is an entity "semitism" that *antisemitism* opposes. In this book, we will follow the IHRA's recommendation.

WHAT IS CHRISTIAN ANTISEMITISM?

When a professing Christian uses the Christian Scriptures to denigrate Jewish people and support antisemitic tropes and conspiracy theories, it is *Christian antisemitism*.

Many Evangelical Christians will argue that there is no such thing as Christian antisemitism. For them, it is a contradiction of terms—an oxymoron. They do not believe a "true" Christian can be antisemitic.

Unfortunately, history has proven otherwise. For example, the father of the Protestant Reformation, Martin Luther, started out as a supporter of the Jews, but when they did not reciprocate by converting to Christianity, he turned against them. His antisemitic book *The Jews and Their Lies* called for synagogues to be burned and sacred books destroyed and for someone to develop a solution to the "devilish burden"—the Jews.

HISTORY OF ANTISEMITISM

The evil pursuit of the Jewish people has continued for millennia, which is why historian Robert Wistrich called antisemitism "the longest hatred." Every time this irrational vitriol seems to be dying out, it reinvents itself with a different look and a different name. But the goal is always the same: to rid the world of the Jewish people.

ANCIENT PAGAN EMPIRES

In the ancient world, antisemitism was a clash between pagan rulers who demanded obedient homage and their Jewish subjects who would only worship and obey the God of Israel. The Jewish people could not bow down to other gods and incurred the wrath of tyrants. The Sinaitic Law also bound them to certain behaviors and observances that set them apart as non-conformist.

This was the situation described in the book of Esther, where Haman, the king's consort, demanded the Jews bow to him, and when they would not, he turned the might of the Persian Empire against them. Hundreds of years later, the Hanukkah story took place under the rule of the Seleucid Emperor Antiochus IV Epiphanes, who attempted to make the Jews into Hellenistic pagans. He banned their religious practices and desecrated their temple resulting in the Maccabean Revolt.

RELIGIOUS ANTISEMITISM

One would think that once paganism gave way to Christianity this problem would go away. Instead, antisemitism took hold in the heart of Christian Europe, and among those who persecuted and hated the Jewish people were professing Christians. Space does not permit a full treatment of this sad story, but anti-Jewish theology led to centuries of church-backed denigration, persecution, forced conversions, and expulsions that paved the way for the Holocaust.

Martin Luther's antisemitic writings were published and distributed by Hitler to justify his treatment of the Jews and their eventual extermination. When two Catholic bishops questioned him about his policy toward the Jews, he replied that he was only putting into effect what Christianity had preached and practiced for 2,000 years.

RACIAL ANTISEMITISM

However, the form of antisemitism found in Nazi ideology was not based on religion but on racial theories promoting the superiority of the Aryan race. In the late nineteenth century, Darwinism was infiltrating the sciences and replacing the God who created the universe with evolution and the idea that man was created in His image with the theory of survival of the fittest. They concluded that the evolution of man was ongoing, and whereas the European people were the most developed, others were inferior and expendable.

Adolf Hitler became an enthusiastic supporter of

Darwin's evil ideas and applied them with fanatical zeal. The German Aryan race was, therefore, at the top of the evolutionary process—and the Jews were at the bottom.

Whereas Christianity had sought the conversion of the Jews and state leaders had sought their expulsion, the Nazis sought the "final solution" to the Jewish problem—the murder of *all* Jews and their eradication from the human race.

POLITICAL ANTISEMITISM: ANTI-ZIONISM

While classical antisemitism blames the Jews for the world's ills, the new antisemitism, called "anti-Zionism," blames the Jewish nation. UCLA Professor Judea Pearl, the father of slain journalist Daniel Pearl, gave this analogy: "Antisemitism rejects the Jews as equal members of the human race; anti-Zionism rejects Israel as an equal member in the family of nations." Believing that the Jewish State (Israel) does not have a right to exist, these enemies of Israel have found a politically correct and sophisticated way to attempt to see the State dismantled.

Not all criticism of Israel can be considered antisemitic. However, criticism of Israel becomes antisemitic when it: 1) delegitimizes the State and questions its right to exist; 2) uses anti-Jewish rhetoric and stereotypes or compares Israelis to Nazis; 3) judges Israel by a different standard than any other nation; or 4) becomes an excuse to attack local Jewish individuals and institutions.

The danger of anti-Zionism was on display during the 2014 war in Gaza (a defensive war on Israel's part to prevent further missile launches from Hamas) when there were attacks on synagogues and Jewish citizens in France. Refrains such as "Jews to the gas" in Germany, the use of swastikas at anti-Israel demonstrations in Latin America, and antisemitic caricatures in Middle Eastern newspapers clearly demonstrated the antisemitic nature of anti-Zionism.

MUSLIM ANTISEMITISM

While anti-Zionism is the new "socially accepted" expression of antisemitism, it is important to note that religious bigotry still exists throughout the Muslim world. Muslims have held negative stereotypes regarding Jews throughout most of Islamic history based on the Quran and Hadith. This theological antisemitism was fertile ground for the racial and militant antisemitism that was transferred to the Islamic world by Nazi leaders during and after World War II and adopted by the jihadist movement birthed then by the Muslim Brotherhood.

Muslim antisemitism is a dangerous mix of religious, racial, and political antisemitism. It is responsible for the genocidal threats against Israel and the United States emanating from jihadist terrorist groups and the Iranian regime. It is a modern-day ideology of hatred and death that must be stopped.

AN EVIL VIRUS

This brief history outlines how antisemitism can be likened to a virus that never entirely dies but mutates and grows again as a new strain in need of new treatments. There is no explanation for this but a biblical one. Antisemitism is, at its root, spiritual—the ugly face of evil.

Psalm 83:1–4 describes it as a war against God in which the Jews are the target:

> Do not keep silent, O God! Do not hold Your peace, and do not be still, O God! For behold, Your enemies make a tumult; and those who hate You have lifted up their head. They have taken crafty counsel against Your people, and consulted together against Your sheltered ones. They have said, "Come,

ANTISEMITISM AND CHRISTIANITY

Jews and Christians have had a history of difficult relations. What started in the first century as an internal squabble amongst Jews over the messiahship of Jesus became a split into two separate religions, both struggling to survive under the brutal Roman Empire.

A CHURCH SEVERED FROM ITS ROOTS

Inevitably, the church became predominantly gentile, made up of pagans who had converted to Christianity with no knowledge of, nor appreciation for, the Jewish roots of the faith or the Jewish people themselves. Several gentile church fathers began to distinguish Christianity by preaching against Judaism and warning their followers away from it.

This is how the teaching of Replacement Theology (also called "supersessionism") took root. Replacement Theology taught that the Jews had been cursed by God for their rejection of Jesus' messianic credentials and had been therefore replaced by the church in the plans and purposes of God.

This theology led to a teaching of contempt for the Jews as "Christ-killers" and gave sanction to their maltreatment.

Once Christianity became the official state religion in the fourth century AD, anti-Jewish theology paved the way for centuries of degrading laws and state-sanctified discrimination, persecution, forced conversions, ghettos, and expulsions of Jews. Centuries of religiously motivated and state-empowered antisemitism prepared the way for the Nazi Holocaust.

To be clear, Christianity did not *cause* the Holocaust. But Christian anti-Judaism, which led to antisemitism—history's oldest hatred—made the Holocaust *possible*. Whereas Christianity had sought the conversion of the Jews and state leaders had sought their expulsion, the Nazis sought the "final solution to the Jewish question": the murder of all Jews and their eradication from the human race.

In recent history, a tectonic shift has taken place within Christianity away from that antisemitic past, and Jewish-Christian relations have never been better than they are today. There are several reasons for this, including the exponential growth of a more Bible-based Christianity over the last several centuries, the harsh lessons learned from the Holocaust, and the exposure of millions of Christians to the Jewish people through tourism to Israel.

Birth of a More Bible-Based Christianity

For most of church history, ordinary Christians did not have access to the Bible to even know what it taught. As a result, there were teachings about the Jewish people that simply were not grounded in Scripture and produced centuries of antisemitism. As soon as the Bible was translated into the vernacular and mass distribution made possible by the printing press, Christians could read the Scriptures for themselves, and many discovered the error of their ways.

They realized that Jesus *was* Jewish and that Christianity had been born out of Judaism. They also read the many promises of God to one day regather the Jewish people back to their ancient homeland. Preachers began to teach about that return, and they prayed for and supported it as an act of justice for a people who had suffered persecution for centuries.

The Holocaust

In addition to access to Scripture, two more recent events brought about significant change in Christian relations with the Jewish people. The first was the Holocaust, which shook the historic churches predominant in Europe.

The Catholic and Lutheran Churches, in particular, reevaluated their theology and liturgy. Some of the most beautiful words of Christian repentance toward the Jewish people ever written are by the Catholic bishops of Europe. While the Catholic Church has sought a new relationship with the Jewish people, they have fallen short of embracing the Jewish State.

The State of Israel

A second event that significantly impacted the Evangelical world was the birth of the State of Israel. This fulfillment of biblical prophecy reinforced God's covenant with the Jewish people and dispelled Replacement Theology. It also allowed millions of Christians to visit Israel to "walk where Jesus walked"—and many interacted with Jewish people for the first time and began to understand the Jewishness of Jesus better. It is no coincidence that over the past four decades, as Christian tourism to Israel has mushroomed, so have Jewish-Christian relations.

While this generation is privileged to be part of a historic correction in the church's relations with the Jews, we cannot take it for granted. Antisemitism is on the rise around the world, and dangerous trends within American churches need addressing to protect this budding relationship. It is the American church that will keep antisemitism from gaining more ground in the country, and it must understand the importance of doing so.

DANGEROUS TRENDS IN CHRISTIANITY TODAY

Most Christians today would never condone the religious antisemitism that fueled centuries of discrimination, persecution, ghettos, and expulsions in the heart of Christian Europe, nor the racial antisemitism embraced by Hitler that led to the horrific genocide campaign known as the Holocaust. But they are vulnerable to the new form of antisemitism that is trying to infiltrate America and Christian churches—anti-Zionism.

Anti-Zionism

Some of the more liberal protestant denominations in America have been passing anti-Israel resolutions calling for divestment from Israel and companies that do business with Israel for years. It should be noted these same liberal Protestant churches are losing members at such an alarming rate that their very survival is questionable.

Within Evangelical ranks, a recent movement to be "pro-Israel, pro-Palestine, pro-peace, and pro-justice" sought to "correct"—or back away—from the pro-Israel movement within Evangelical Christianity and entertain an anti-Israel narrative under the banner of "love and peace" for all. While the effects of this movement have been limited at the grassroots level, a similar reaction took place in seminaries and Christian colleges, creating a new generation of pastors and Christian leaders who do not want to be associated with support of Israel.

Two other dangerous trends in the American church are making it increasingly vulnerable to antisemitic narratives against Israel and the Jewish people: a loss of biblical literacy and rising Replacement Theology.

Loss of Biblical Literacy

While Evangelical Christianity—and its inherent support for Israel—is mushrooming in Asia, Africa, and Latin America, it has plateaued in the United States (and Europe) and is losing its momentum. This is evident in the growing biblical illiteracy in society, not to mention prominent Evangelical voices challenging core biblical tenets and the Bible itself.

One prominent Evangelical pastor with a huge following has publicly discounted the Old Testament and blamed it for the loss of faith in the younger generation. When the Old Testament is discarded, God's covenant with the Jewish people and the biblical significance of modern Israel goes with it.

Rising Replacement Theology

In this atmosphere of questioning—even disregarding—the Old Testament, Replacement Theology is gaining traction under various names and guises, one of which is Fulfillment Theology. Jesus said He did not come to abolish the law but to fulfill it (Matthew 5:17). However, Fulfillment Theology maintains that Jesus' fulfillment *did* abolish the law and, with it, God's covenantal relationship with Israel. It also teaches that all Old Testament promises to Israel are fulfilled in Jesus; thus, they are no longer valid regarding modern Israel.

Although this view may lack the same degree

of animus toward the Jews as historical anti-Jewish preaching, Fulfillment Theology still winds up in the same place as Replacement Theology—namely that God is finished with the Jewish people and has replaced them with the church.

It is important to clarify that just because someone holds a form of Replacement or Fulfillment Theology does not mean that they are antisemitic. Many well-meaning pastors hold replacement views more as a theological assumption simply because they were never taught otherwise.

Replacement Theology, however, robs Christians of the very root that sustains our faith and separates us from the people who represent the truth of the Bible and the faithfulness of God to always keep His word. As the apostle Paul said, it is the Jewish faith that is the root that supports us (Romans 11:18). To be separated from that root means spiritual death. It also leaves Christians vulnerable to anti-Israel and antisemitic sentiments. If we believe the Jews were bad enough to have lost their standing with God, then we may believe the worst of accusations any antisemite might bring forward.

The battle against this dangerous ideology is *our* battle. It behooves us to do everything we can to help churches recognize it for what it is and stand against it.

CONCLUSION

Jewish-Christian relations have never been better, and churches around the world are standing with Israel and the Jewish people. Thankfully, Christian antisemites are few and far between and are largely condemned by the Evangelical world, which is the fastest-growing segment of Christianity and soon to be the largest.

However, the liberalization of Evangelical churches in America and the rise of theologies that spiritualize or discount the Old Testament is disturbing. These trends leave the Evangelical church in America increasingly vulnerable to the antisemitism seeping into our schools and society.

ANTISEMITISM IN THE UNITED STATES

A recent study found a startling 85 percent of Americans—as many as 285 million people—believe at least one anti-Jewish trope,[5] as opposed to 61 percent in 2019, and 20 percent of Americans believe six or more tropes, up from 11 percent in 2019, the highest rate since the early 1990s.[6] The January 2023 study published by The London Centre for the Study of Contemporary Antisemitism in partnership with the Anti-Defamation League and the National Opinion Research Center at the University of Chicago also revealed "widespread belief in antisemitic conspiracy theories and tropes (20 percent)—nearly doubling the antisemitic prejudice ADL found in 2019—as well as substantially negative anti-Israel sentiment among Americans."[7]

---

[5] An antisemitic trope is a myth or sensational report, misrepresentation, or fabrication defamatory toward Judaism or the Jewish people as an ethnic or religious group. Some tropes date back to the birth of Christianity, like the belief that Jews are collectively responsible for Jesus' crucifixion. Other antisemitic tropes include the ideas that the Jews control the media and the global financial system with the goal of world domination, that they are profiteers and spies, and that they perform ritual murder or "blood libel."

[6] Ibid.

[7] *American Defamation League*, "*Report: Antisemitic Attitudes in America: Topline Findings*," 12 January 2023.

Antisemitism is now seeping into the United States via college campuses, where Palestinian groups are mobilizing students to their cause by using anti-Israel vitriol. A frightening alliance of these anti-Israel groups with progressives and far right activists has made campuses dangerous for anyone Jewish or pro-Israel.

Another frontier for the spread of antisemitism is the internet, where hate-filled people spew a relentless stream of paranoia and lies inciting some to acts of violence. That is how Robert Bowers was incited to take a semi-automatic weapon into the Tree of Life Synagogue in Pittsburgh in 2018 to kill as many Jews as possible.

ANTI-ZIONISM

Since a Jewish nation-state is antithetical to the ruling philosophies of our day—globalism and secularism—this modern form of political antisemitism is finding large-scale acceptance. It is directed not at individual Jews but against the collective Jew—the Jewish State—and is called anti-Zionism.

Natan Sharansky, an Israeli politician and human rights activist who spent nine years in a USSR gulag for being a Zionist, developed the 3D test to determine when discussion of Israel is antisemitic. If any of the following are true—delegitimization of Israel, demonization of Israel, or subjecting Israel to a double standard—criticism of Israel is antisemitic.

IHRA's working definition of antisemitism also includes examples of antisemitic anti-Zionism:

- Denying the Jewish people their right to self-determination, e.g., by claiming that the existence of a State of Israel is a racist endeavor

- Applying double standards by requiring a behavior

not expected or demanded of any other democratic nation

- Using the symbols and images associated with classic antisemitism (e.g., claims of Jews killing Jesus or blood libel) to characterize Israel or Israelis

- Drawing comparisons of contemporary Israeli policy to that of the Nazis

- Holding Jews collectively responsible for actions of the State of Israel

BDS MOVEMENT

The Boycott, Divestment, and Sanctions (BDS) movement unfairly places blame on Israel, then calls for others to boycott, divest from, or sanction the Jewish State. A central premise of the BDS movement is that modern Israel is a racist reincarnation of apartheid South Africa. Ignoring Palestinian demands for a Jew-free state, BDS activists paint Israel as an "apartheid state" that employs "Nazi-like" policies against the Palestinian people. They boycott corporations operating in Israel, stores selling Israeli products, entertainers who plan performances in Israel, and Israeli academic institutions.

The BDS National Committee (BNC) was established in 2007 in Ramallah from where the Palestinian coordinating body manages the international campaign. Their aim has nothing to do with creating conditions on the ground where Israelis and Palestinians can finally live side by side in peace and prosperity. On the contrary, it opposes any peace efforts between Israel and the Palestinians. The final solution the BDS movement ultimately seeks is the complete dismantling of the Jewish State to be replaced with a Palestinian State.

COLLEGE CAMPUSES

Hostility toward Israel's supporters on campus has reached near-historic levels. According to a December 2022 AMCHA Initiative executive summary report:

> Attacks on Jewish student identity—including well-coordinated campaigns of vilification using classic antisemitic tropes of Jewish power, control, and privilege carried out by students and professors alike—doubled this year [2022] on campuses across the country. Whether the source of the antisemitism emanates from the right, in the form of classic antisemitism, or from the left, in the form of anti-Zionism, the rhetoric used to portray Jews is becoming increasingly similar. While they direct their bigotry to different audiences, their intended effect is the same: to portray Jews as a threat to the common good, whose malevolent influence must be challenged and neutralized.[8]

The AMCHA Initiative states that attempts to exclude Jewish and pro-Israel students from campus activities more than doubled, "with expression calling for the total boycott or exclusion of pro-Israel students from campus life nearly tripling."

A November 2022 report from the AMCHA Initiative documents that in the 2021–2022 academic year, "incidents involving the suppression, denigration, or challenges to the definition of Jewish identity were found on nearly 60 percent of the campuses most popular with Jewish students."[9]

---

[8] AMCHA Initiative, "Falling through the Cracks: How School Policies Deny Jewish Students," amchainitiative.org, December 2022.

[9] AMCHA Initiative, *Assault on Jewish Identity Report*, amchainitiative.org. AMCHA Initiative is a nonpartisan organization whose sole mission is to document, investigate, and combat antisemitism on US college campuses. AMCHA uses the International Holocaust Remembrance Alliance (IHRA) and US State Department definitions to identify incidents of antisemitism.

A statement released by Alums for Campus Fairness on September 22, 2022, reveals that 98.2 percent of the articles published about Israel in 75 college newspapers from 2017 to 2022 were heavily biased against Israel.[10] And a spring 2021 report from the Brandeis Center demonstrates that because of pervasive antisemitism on campus—even amid the pandemic—50 percent of Jewish students hid their Jewish identity, and more than half did not express views on Israel.[11]

A 2019 report by the Institute for the Global Study of Antisemitism and Policy (ISGAP) describes one of the most active antisemitic forces on campuses, National Students for Justice in Palestine (NSJP), whose goal is the elimination of the State of Israel.

FAR LEFT AND FAR RIGHT

Whereas the BDS movement is largely a progressive liberal movement of advocates involved in numerous causes, such as human rights, gender equality, and abortion, these liberal activists are finding common causes with white supremacists, fascists, and the remnants of the neo-Nazi movement.

That common goal is the demonization of Jews.

The growing number of young progressives taking leadership in the Democratic Party has brought antisemitic tropes and conspiracies to mainstream political discourse. On the other extreme, white supremacists are now adopting and promoting the BDS campaign's antisemitic propaganda and imagery.

---

10 *ALUMS for Campus Fairness*, "New ACF Report Exposes Institutional Bias at Campus Newspapers," 22 September 2022.

11 Louis D. Brandeis Center for Human Rights under Law, "Survey: Anti-Semitism at College," spring 2021.

THE INTERNET

The problem of antisemitism in the United States is a problem of the far left and far right fringes and not one of mainstream society. However, social media and communication technologies that bypass conventional media controls have allowed the fringe to have excessive influence and to network with each other in unprecedented and alarming ways. Rumors and conspiracy theories can now spread around the globe in seconds on the internet.

CONSPIRACY THEORIES AND PANDEMICS

Pandemics are dangerous times for Jewish communities due to the conspiracy theories they spawn. One of the greatest catastrophes to afflict humanity was the fourteenth-century bubonic plague—known as the "Black Death"—that swept through Europe. Historians estimate that up to 50 percent of Europe's population died in the pandemic, with rates of death as high as 75 percent in Italy, Spain, and France.

Church and state had already demonized the Jewish minority, so they were an easy scapegoat. They also fared better than the general population, possibly due to their dietary and religious practices or the fact many were confined in walled ghettos. Their lower death rates, however, fueled suspicions they were behind the pandemic, and many Jews who survived the plague were then massacred in pogroms.

During the COVID crisis of 2020, antisemites spread lies that Jews developed the virus to kill many people and gain power. They were also accused of using it to make money selling the antidote. The fact that the Orthodox Jewish community in New York had higher rates of infection than the general population was used as proof. The lies were propagated on all social media platforms.

We should not dismiss conspiracy theories as mere

craziness. Conspiracy theories produce anger, and anger moves quickly from words into actions; verbal insults often result in physical attacks.

HOLOCAUST DENIAL

Holocaust denial is any attempt to diminish or deny the established facts of the Nazi genocide of European Jews. This is a form of antisemitism because it perpetuates the antisemitic trope that Jews are dishonest and manipulative and accuses them of inventing or exaggerating the Holocaust as a plot to advance "Jewish interests."

Some common Holocaust denials include reducing the number of Jews who were murdered in the Holocaust; denying the existence of Nazi facilities that used gas chambers to systematically murder Jews; and denying the widespread killing of Jews in *all* the camps—not just in ones equipped with a means of mass extermination.

Many Americans have fathers or grandfathers who fought in World War II and may have personally witnessed the carnage the Nazis left behind in the camps. Holocaust denial is not only an affront to the Jewish people but to all those who fought to bring down the evil Nazi regime.

CONCLUSION

A 2023 public opinion survey by the American Jewish Committee (AJC) revealed that after the 2022 hostage situation at a synagogue in Colleyville, Texas, US Jews feel less secure. In its first-ever *State of Antisemitism in America* report, released in 2020, the AJC found 88 percent of Jewish Americans believe antisemitism is a problem, and over the past five years, 82 percent believe antisemitism in the

United States has increased.[12]

While there is a combination of reasons for the increase, there is one thing that can stop it.

One of the largest demographics in America—Evangelical Christians—must be educated to recognize antisemitism in all its forms and stand against its spread into society. If the Holocaust taught us anything, it is that a silent majority is an enabling majority. Christians in the United States must learn to speak out while they can.

---

[12] American Jewish Committee, "The State of Antisemitism in America 2020: The AJC's Survey of American Jews," 2020.

WHAT CAN YOU DO?

Much can and should be done. While this chapter cannot provide an exhaustive list, let's concentrate on the most obvious things that most of us can do at the community level.

- Reach out to your local Jewish community or one that has suffered an antisemitic attack. Let them know how sorry you are and that you are praying for them. You can do this by sending a card to the rabbi or the Jewish Federation director in that city. Showing up at a local memorial service speaks louder than words. Do not come with an agenda or message other than "we are sorry."

- Holocaust Survivor Elie Wiesel once wrote: "What hurts the victim most is not the cruelty of the oppresor but the silence of the bystander." We are often silent because we do not know what to say, but your silence is deafening in times of grief. Please voice your condolence.

- If you come across ugly comments on the internet, call them out for being antisemitic so others who encounter this will be alerted. The first step in opposing this evil is identifying it for what it is. Learn how to combat the lies permeating the internet so that it becomes a place of pushing back against the hatred. Visit the Israel Answers website at www.israelanswers.com for teachings and answers to frequently asked questions.

- If you are an alumnus of a college or university, contact the school president and let them know how concerned you are about this issue, and ask what they are doing about it. Suggest they include courses against movements of hate, including antisemitism; monitor anti-Israel groups calling for "death to Israel" and "death to Zionists"; and take seriously any complaints of antisemitism by their Jewish students.

- Help inform and educate your church about the history and current expressions of antisemitism. The International Christian Embassy Jerusalem (ICEJ) provides informative seminars that do this from a biblical perspective. These seminars are enlightening and inspire churches to take a stance on behalf of the Jewish people.

These are simple steps that most of us can take. If we focus on the local level and within our sphere of influence, we can each make a small difference—and that can add up to a whole lot of good.

International Christian Embassy Jerusalem

The birth of the International Christian Embassy Jerusalem (ICEJ) in 1980 was a historic, groundbreaking moment. For the first time in history, Christians were mobilizing support for the Jewish people on an international scale and from Jerusalem—the capital of the newborn State of Israel. While 2,000 years of history cannot be changed overnight, the ICEJ has had the privilege of confronting this history and establishing a new relationship with the Jewish people.

The ICEJ headquarters in Jerusalem carries out projects to bless Israel on behalf of millions of Christians worldwide. Our branches and representatives in over 90 countries help the worldwide body of Christ come to a greater understanding of this unique land and people.

Through the ICEJ's partnership with Yad Vashem—Israel's Holocaust memorial and remembrance center—we educate Christians on the Holocaust and antisemitism.

ICEJ USA provides educational tools to churches and individuals including:

- Half-day seminars designed to educate and inspire
- Speakers for churches and events
- Online courses available at www.iceju.org
- Israel Answers website—the Christian community's most extensive resource on Israel, antisemitism, and Christian Zionism
- American Christian Leaders for Israel (ACLI) network to educate and mobilize Christian leaders

To get involved, please contact us at:

ICEJ USA • PO Box 332974 • Murfreesboro, TN 37133-2974
(615) 895-9830 • info@icejusa.org • www.icejusa.org

RESOURCES

ORGANIZATIONS

- Combat Antisemitism Movement (CAM)—CAM is a global network of organizations and individuals committed to confronting antisemitism and provides excellent weekly recaps of antisemitism around the world.

- The Anti-Defamation League (ADL)—The mission of ADL is to stop the defamation of the Jewish people and to secure justice and fair treatment to all.

- The AMCHA Initiative—AMCHA Initiative is a nonprofit organization dedicated to investigating, documenting, educating about, and combating antisemitism at institutions of higher education in America.

PAPERS

- "The New Anti-Semites" by StopAntisemitism.org and Zachor Legal Institute

- "NSJP Threat to Academic Freedom" by igap.org

BOOKS

- Bernard Lewis, *Semites and Anti-Semites: An Inquiry into Conflict and Prejudice*, W. Norton & Company, 2014.

- Raul Hilberg, *The Destruction of the European Jews*, Martino Fine Books, 2019 Reprint of 1961 Edition.

- Dennis Prager and Joseph Telushkin, *Why the Jews?* Touchstone, 2003.

- Deborah Lipstadt, *Antisemitism: Here and Now*, Schocken, 2019.

- Eric Rozenman, *Jews Make the Best Demons: "Palestine" and the Jewish Question*, New English Review Press, 2018.

- Alan Dershowitz, *The Case against BDS: Why Singling Out Israel for Boycott Is Antisemitic and Anti-Peace*, Post Hill Press, 2018.

- Stephen Norwood, *Antisemitism and the American Far Left*, Cambridge University Press, 2013.

- Neil Kressel, *"The Sons of Pigs and Apes": Muslim Antisemitism and the Conspiracy of Silence*, Potomac Books, 2012.

- Edward H. Flannery, *The Anguish of the Jews*, Macmillan, 1965.

- Michael L. Brown, *Christian Antisemitism*, Charisma House, February 2, 2021.

- Michael L. Brown, *Our Hands Are Stained with Blood*, Destiny Image Publishers, 1992, Revised and Expanded, 2019.

GET YOUR FREE RESOURCE TODAY

Request your FREE downloadable resource *10 Reasons Christians Should Stand with Israel*—and share it with family and friends. This full-color resource includes vibrant pictures and 10 biblical reasons why we should support, bless, and stand with God's chosen people, the Jews. You'll also be alerted when we release a new book, online course, or other educational tools!

GET YOUR FREE RESOURCE TODAY
by going to: www.icejusa.org/10reasons

LEARN MORE ABOUT OTHER RESOURCES
by Dr. Susan Michael at: www.susanmichael.com

LEARN MORE ABOUT THE MINISTRY
of the International Christian Embassy Jerusalem at:
www.icejusa.org

FOLLOW US ON
www.facebook.com/icejusa
www.instagram.com/icejusa_1980

LEARN MORE ABOUT
ICEJ U online courses, books, and podcasts at:
www.iceju.org

CONTACT US AT
embassy.publishers@icejusa.org

ABOUT ▪▪▪
DR. SUSAN MICHAEL

For more than 35 years, Susan has pioneered the development of the International Christian Embassy Jerusalem in the United States and around the world. She currently serves as the ministry's USA Director and is a member of the ICEJ's international Board of Directors. In addition to a master's degree in Judeo-Christian Studies from the Jerusalem University College, she holds a bachelor's degree in theology from Oral Roberts University and was awarded an Honorary Doctorate of Laws by Piedmont International University in 2018. Susan is an author, gifted teacher, and international speaker.

She is often called upon to address complex and sensitive issues, such as antisemitism, Jewish-Christian relations, Christian Zionism, and current events in the Middle East to a diverse range of audiences. Her experience working with Jews, Christians, and Arabs from many national and denominational backgrounds has equipped her to handle delicate topics central to an understanding of Israel with extraordinary clarity and grace.

In recent years she has produced several educational tools to enable other Christians to do the same, including the ICEJ U online school, the IsraelAnswers.com website, biblical study tours to Israel through ICEJ USA Tours, and Susan's Blog of over 200 articles and podcasts. Susan has built the US Branch of the ICEJ into a scripturally sound, balanced, and reputable ministry, evidenced in its leadership of one of the strongest networks of Evangelical leaders in America—the American Christian Leaders for Israel (ACLI).

Made in the USA
Las Vegas, NV
18 January 2024